MOTIVATION & CONCENTRATION

"Learn How To Learn"
STUDY SKILLS

By

Herman Ohme, Ed.D.

Published By

CALIFORNIA EDUCATION PLAN, INC.
4074 Fabian Way • Palo Alto, CA 94303

Motivation & Concentration
Copyright ©1987 by Herman Ohme
First Printing 1987
Second Printing 1989

All rights reserved. No part of this publication may be reproduced, stored in a retrieval system, or transcribed in any form, or by any means without prior written permission of the publisher, CALIFORNIA EDUCATION PLAN, Inc.

ISBN 0-936047-01-1

Printed in the United States of America

10 9 8 7 6 5 4 3 2

Cover Design by Rogondino & Associates

ABOUT THE AUTHOR

Herman Ohme, Ed.D., is an expert in the field of SCHOOL PERFORMANCE, LEARNING, and MOTIVATION. He has taught at U.C.L.A., Yale, and Stanford, and has been a teacher, counselor, and administrator in public and private schools for over 20 years. He is currently devoting full time to consultation, writing, and speaking on the subject of "Learn How To Learn" STUDY SKILLS.

TABLE OF CONTENTS

Motivation	1
Goals and Goal Setting	2
Purpose	11
The Personal Values Inventory	12
Self Initiation	16
Concentration	19
Purpose and Practicality	20
Interest	25
Control	29
Consequence I-If Nothing Else Works	34
Consequence II-Success Becomes A Habit	35

1
MOTIVATION

"Get what you like, or like what you get"
(George Bernard Shaw)

Motivation is a power source that helps you find or make the "circumstances" you want. It fires you up. It gets you going and keeps you going until you reach your goal. Where does that power or energy come from? How do you get it? How do you use it? How do you hold on to it so that you always have it when you need it? Why do some people have so much more than others? Do only smart people get motivated? If people are smart, do they have to be motivated?

Suppose we look at **MOTIVATION** in relation to what you do every day in school, and how you can become *motivated* in order to get what you want out of school, and out of life.

There are three basic parts to **MOTIVATION:**

•*GOAL SETTING.* *What* do you want to achieve? This is the end point, but unless you have some idea of *what* you want, there is little you can do to become motivated. Before you start out on a trip, you have to know where you want to go, or what the end point will be.

•*PURPOSE.* Now that you know what you want, you will have a greater chance of getting it if you know *why* you want it. While the goal was the "end point," the *purpose* is the reason. Goals without a clearly defined *purpose* are seldom fulfilled. For example, suppose your goal is "to become a millionaire" before you reach the age of 21. A lot of people have goals to "get rich." There is nothing wrong with wanting to "get rich." It is a legitimate goal, provided there is a purpose. Why become a millionaire before the age of 21? Without sitting in judgment about whether the reason is right or wrong, the goal will remain a fantasy if it has no purpose and is not connected to the goal.

•*SELF INITIATION*. You have a goal; you know the reason (purpose) for the goal; now all you need is the "fuel" or energy to reach the goal. What do you do to reach your goal? How do you get started and keep going? You can certainly understand that simply "putting fuel in the tank" won't necessarily get you anywhere. But once you know where and why you are going, it then is up to you to arrange to get there. More on this later.

The three parts of **MOTIVATION** are like the legs of a three-legged stool: take any one away and the stool falls. Each is equally important. It does no good to have goals without a purpose, and even with a goal and the best reason in the world, if you can't get yourself going, you might as well forget the whole thing. Let's look at the three parts of **MOTIVATION** in greater detail.

Goals and Goal Setting

Goals are best described in terms of **RANGE**, the length of time it takes to reach the goal; and **CLASSIFICATION**, the priority or importance of each of your goals.

RANGE

There are three:

- *Short*, concerns the here and now.

- *Intermediate*, is several months to several years.

- *Long*, usually deals with lifetime and career.

Review the following information on goal characteristics, and think of where you would place most of your goals.

Short. The most significant characteristic here is the need for some sort of **immediate gratification**. You want results *now*, not next week or next month. Students whose goals are mostly in this range would have few plans for what they intend to do after they graduate from high school. They also may respond in extremes to the way they feel about a teacher, or the way they think a teacher feels about them.

When I ask a student about an occasional high grade among mostly poor grades, they are inclined to say that they happened to like that particular teacher. Conversely, there are many teachers they did not like, or who they feel did not like them. These students are unmotivated in terms of goal setting, and they are on a perpetually moving carousel of short range needs that require immediate gratification.

I hope you don't get the notion that *short range* goals are bad. Not true! We all have them. The point I would stress is that when a student's goals are practically all limited to short range, then what I have stated in the previous paragraph tends to be valid. But how do you begin to reverse this pattern?

The first step is to become more *realistic* when setting short range goals. The key word is "realistic."

It removes goal setting from the world of immediate gratification and fantasy. There are two *"musts"* for making short range goals realistic and effective:

- Goals *must* be *achievable*.

- *Outcomes* must be clearly stated and understood.

An achievable realistic short range goal should be accomplished without interference or unnecessary delay. These goals should be task-oriented which means "doing" rather than thought-oriented which means "thinking" or "fantasizing" about doing. Following are examples of task oriented short range goals:

- *Complete* a homework assignment due the following day

- *Prepare* for a spelling test

- *Memorize* ten Spanish vocabulary words

Each of these can be done in a short time. Each is "achievable," clearly stated, and most important of all, each is associated with a "realistic" outcome that will soon occur. The homework assignment is due the following day; the spelling test will likely take place on the next day; the Spanish vocabulary words are in the daily lesson.

I am certain you have noted that these goals are all connected with school work. Why would a student who rarely ever does any school work decide to do a homework assignment, prepare for a spelling test, or memorize Spanish vocabulary words?

Here is where the "achievable" notion becomes all important. Start with whatever piece of the task you might be willing to undertake. Something is better than nothing. If the homework assignment is eight pages of United States History, even two pages would be better than nothing. Half the spelling words would be better than none, and the same for half or any part of the Spanish vocabulary words.

You wonder how a piecemeal approach can accomplish anything. You will still be unprepared. Your grades will still be low. Your performance will be below minimum standards. What good will it do?

Remember, we are trying to move beyond "immediate gratification" to some sort of realistic goal setting. It is almost impossible to make the jump in one leap. It will have to happen gradually, in short steps.

The value of the small first step is that the step has been made. It should set the stage for the next step. If good notes are taken on the two pages of United States History, then you will retain something, and hopefully a new pattern of goal setting performance will have begun.

I also suggest that when moving from "immediate gratification" to short range realistic goals, you speak with your teachers about what you are doing. You will need their cooperation and assistance.

Intermediate. For these goals the time span is from a few months to several years. It requires a longer period of waiting for results or gratification. Students who set goals in this range are more concerned about the quality of their work than whether the teacher likes them, or if they like the teacher.

These require planning and preparation. Nothing is left to chance. There are specific activities, tasks, problems to be solved and things to be accomplished if these goals are to be achieved. When you can set intermediate range goals and follow through, with everything required, you are a candidate for success. You know what you want, and are willing to do what it takes to get it.

Long. These are the big ones. What do you want to do with your life? Do you want to be the president of a large corporation? A professional tennis player? Write a great (best seller) novel?

Although this type of goal may not be too important to you at this time, you should be able to give some thought to any possible long range goals you may think of. As you get older, your goals will undoubtedly change. That is quite natural.

CLASSIFICATION OF GOALS

All goals are not the same. Some are more important than others. Earning a varsity letter is not in the same category as getting into a "good" college. (Are there any "bad" colleges?) Goals are best ranked as follows:

    A - *Most Important*

    B - *Important*

    C - *Least Important*

On the following page are examples of ***short***, ***intermediate***, and ***long range*** goals, and the priorities given them by three different students. What can you assume about these students from the priorities they set?

	Priority For Student		
SHORT RANGE GOALS	#1	#2	#3
Go on a ski trip next weekend	A	B	B
Read a good book	C	B	A
Receive a good grade on a test in Algebra	B	A	A
Get a new outfit for the prom	B	B	C
Go to a party on the weekend	A	B	C
INTERMEDIATE RANGE GOALS			
Get into a good college	B	A	A
Save enough money to buy a bicycle	A	A	B
Earn a varsity letter	C	B	B
Spend the summer in Mexico	C	B	C
Become an Eagle Scout	C	B	A
Get a summer apprenticeship at IBM	C	C	A
LONG RANGE GOALS			
Become an airline pilot	C	B	C
Do "life saving" research	C	C	A
Make lots of money	A	A	B
Own a yacht	B	C	C
Become a senator	C	C	C
Retire by age 40	A	B	C
Create something new and original	C	C	A

Notice where the higher priorities are. Next, eliminate all the <u>C</u> GOALS, and examine what remains. See the following page.

Notice the priorities without <u>C</u> GOALS.

SHORT RANGE GOALS	Priority For Student #1	#2	#3
Go on a ski trip next weekend	A	B	B
Read a good book		B	A
Receive a good grade on a test in Algebra	B	A	A
Get a new outfit for the prom	B	B	
Go to a party on the weekend	A	B	

INTERMEDIATE RANGE GOALS

	#1	#2	#3
Get into a good college	B	A	A
Save enough money to buy a bicycle	A	A	B
Earn a varsity letter		B	B
Spend the summer in Mexico		B	
Become an Eagle Scout		B	A
Get a summer apprenticeship at IBM			A

LONG RANGE GOALS

	#1	#2	#3
Become an airline pilot		B	
Do "life saving" research			A
Make lots of money	A	A	B
Own a yacht	B		
Become a senator	C		
Retire by age 40	A	B	
Create something new and original			A

Read the analysis on the next page. Do you agree with my interpretation?

Student #1 has a cluster of short range goals that provide clues about what he thinks is most important and also how he prefers to spend his time. His intermediate range goals show a type of "lip service" regarding his going to college. His long range goals have an element of fantasy about them when we see the inconsistency with his short and intermediate range goals.

Student #2 has fairly well balanced short and intermediate range goals. He wants to enjoy himself, but he also thinks beyond the immediate present. His long range goals have little substance. Viewed alone, they would be cause for concern, but not so when we look at his other priorities.

Student #3 is the serious member of the group. His priorities at every range are consistent with what I would consider strong purpose and dedication. In my opinion, there is a hint of potential anxiety. I would want to look more deeply at his background and former records to determine if this is true. He doesn't seem to have much fun. He seems highly driven to perform and prepare for the future. I would wonder how much of this is for himself, or how much is an effort to please others.

What we don't know from examining the priorities is how much effort the students will put forth to achieve their <u>A</u> goals.

It is now time for you to look at your own goals and priorities. On the next page, write down as many of your short, intermediate, and long range goals as possible. List the first ones that come to mind; don't edit them. You can do that later. Use more paper if necessary. Then classify all the goals as <u>A</u>, <u>B</u>, or <u>C</u>. After you finish, look over what you have done and take out whatever you feel does not belong. Keep the list and edit it from time to time. Think of what you need to do to achieve your <u>A</u> and <u>B</u> goals.

GOAL SETTING EXERCISE

SHORT RANGE   **PRIORITY**

1. _____ A___ B___ C___

2. _____ A___ B___ C___

3. _____ A___ B___ C___

4. _____ A___ B___ C___

INTERMEDIATE RANGE

1. _____ A___ B___ C___

2. _____ A___ B___ C___

3. _____ A___ B___ C___

4. _____ A___ B___ C___

LONG RANGE

1. _____ A___ B___ C___

2. _____ A___ B___ C___

3. _____ A___ B___ C___

4. _____ A___ B___ C___

Purpose

It is not enough to simply *want* something (goal). You have to know *why (purpose)* you want it. You have to have a reason, and the reason has to be "legitimate." Otherwise you are living in a world of fantasy. For example, suppose your goal (in this case - long range) is "to be rich and famous." It already sounds like a fantasy! If I ask you what the possible reasons are, you might say that:

- You could then have everything you want.
- Everyone would want your autograph.
- You could help the poor people.
- You would't have to work.

Ridiculous, you say. But how many people do you know who think that way? Why are lotteries and other types of gambling so popular? What chance is there to be a winner? Why do they keep trying? Is it "human nature?"

Whatever it is, it may *not* be an attainable goal. The reason is because the *purpose* is unrealistic. It doesn't stand up well even as a fantasy. Let's look at some other examples.

You want to be admitted to the University of California at Los Angeles. This would be an intermediate range goal, with undoubtedly an A priority. *Why* do you want to go to the University of California (or a comparable university)?

The reason is that U. C. L. A. has an excellent program in Biology, and one of your long range goals is to become a biologist. Note how the reason to attend U. C. L. A. applies to both of your goals. You have a "legitimate" purpose in wanting to go to U. C. L. A.

Your intermediate range goals require a lot of short range goals to help you get where you want to go. Once you have set the University of California goal, then your day to day work at school becomes more *purposeful*. Why? Because it will all help you achieve your University of California goal.

Suppose, however, you had a goal of being admitted to the University of California, Santa Barbara. When I ask you why, your answer is that you want to be near the ocean because you like to surf. What do you think I would say? If this is your only reason for going there, what do you think your chances for admission would be? If you were admitted, what would have to happen for you to succeed there?

THE PERSONAL VALUES INVENTORY

As you think about your beliefs and values, you get closer to what *purpose* is all about. It is not my intent to be the judge of those values. That is for you to decide. However, it is important to clarify your values, your beliefs, and how they relate to your goals. Use the following check list as a starting point, and make your own additions, or modifications as you see fit. The Inventory consists of three parts: **Family**, **School**, and **Vocation**. Answer True, False, or Not Applicable to each of the statements.

Family

T F NA   1. I enjoy spending time with my parents.

T F NA   2. I enjoy spending time with my brother(s) and sister(s).

T F NA 3. I feel I take more than my share of the responsibilities at home.

T F NA 4. I ought to help make the decisions that affect me or our family.

T F NA 5. I usually agree with what my parents expect.

T F NA 6. I often disagree with my parents "old fashioned" ideas, but I don't argue about it.

T F NA 7. I don't expect to make the same mistakes my parents made when I become an adult.

T F NA 8. My parents ideas don't ever seem to change.

T F NA 9. I am proud of my parents accomplishments.

T F NA 10. I value the advice I get from my parents.

School

T F NA 1. The main reason I go to school is to learn.

T F NA 2. I would transfer to any school that my friends attended.

T F NA 3. I work harder for teachers I like.

T F NA 4. I respect teachers who have high standards.

T   F   NA   5. Whenever possible, I select teachers who have the highest standards.

T   F   NA   6. The grade I get is the most important part of the course.

T   F   NA   7. I have good reasons to be proud of my school.

T   F   NA   8. I am actively involved in my school.

T   F   NA   9. Most of my teachers care a lot about me.

T   F   NA   10. Most of my friends work hard at school and get good grades.

Vocation

T   F   NA   1. I think a lot about what I would like to do after I leave school.

T   F   NA   2. I am interested in jobs that pay a lot.

T   F   NA   3. I like working with people.

T   F   NA   4. I expect the work I do to be more important than how much I earn.

T   F   NA   5. I have some general ideas about what I would like to do, but I think it's too early to be specific.

T   F   NA   6. I would like to take a year off after I graduate from high school so I can get a better idea of what I would like to do with my life.

T   F   NA   7. The most important thing about school or college is the diploma.

T   F   NA   8. "The harder I work, the luckier I get." Quote by John Wooden, former basketball coach at U. C. L. A.

T   F   NA   9. The more I learn, the more confident I become.

T   F   NA   10. My ambition is to be #1 when I do something I really like.

After you respond to these statements, you should have a fairly good view of your personal values as they relate to your idea of *purpose.*

15

Self Initiation

How do you get yourself started, and once started, how do you keep going and maintain momentum. Obviously, you start with a goal and a purpose for having the goal. *Plan* what you have to do to achieve the goal. First you *plan*, then you *implement* the plan--a fancy way to say "get the job done."

PLANNING

Planning to achieve intermediate or longer range goal involves **strategy**. Look for the most direct routes or means to reach your goal. It has to be done long enough in advance to avoid any type of potential problem. For example, your goal is to attend an Ivy League college such as Stanford, or Princeton. That goal should be set no later than your first year in high school.

The strategy (strategic plan) is to acquire broad knowledge, get outstanding grades, develop any other skills that interest you such as sports, music, drama, journalism, or student government. At the same time, you will need to develop good relationships with your counselor, school administrators, and teachers. They are the ones who can give you the recommendations you will need to compete with other outstanding students from all over the country.

Does this sound hypocritical, phoney, or what some people call "opportunistic?" Maybe so, especially if your purpose is a bit foggy. But if you want to go to a University like Stanford because you believe that the preparation at Stanford will be the most challenging and thorough, then there is nothing, in my opinion, "opportunistic" about your strategic plannning. If you want to go to Stanford because you expect to meet and marry someone rich and socially prominent, then your efforts (which may get you there) are, in my opinion, "opportunistic," (phoney).

You can apply the same strategic planning to almost any of your goals. It is the starting point, and the closer you adhere to the plan, the more likely you will be to reach the goal. Next, however, is the most difficult part: making the plan work.

IMPLEMENTING YOUR PLAN

Once you decide where you are going and how you plan to get there, then everything you do must get you closer to that goal. With a goal like getting into a University such as Stanford, start early, and monitor yourself all the way. It means studying, participating, building skills, and developing, confidence, good relationships, and good insight into yourself. It is a difficult goal and one with a certain amount of risk. Remember this: the harder you work the more confident you become, and the lower the risk becomes.

"Mabel, I just can't stick to a diet the way you do!"

Motivation - Chapter Summary

There are three parts to **MOTIVATION**:

- *Goal* Setting.
- *Purpose.*
- *Self Initiation.*

GOALS have *RANGE*, and *CLASSIFICATION*. The *RANGES* are:

- *Short*: up to a few months.
- *Intermediate*: up to a few years.
- *Long*: career and life.

CLASSIFICATION or *PRIORITY* has three levels:

A - *Most Important*

B - *Important*

C - *Least Important*

PURPOSE is your *reason* for having a goal.

SELF INITIATION is the *energy* needed to achieve your goals.

2

CONCENTRATION
"Concentration is mental magic"

If there is one single skill that students find difficult to master, it is the skill of **concentration**: how to get started and focus on an assignment until it is done. How do you avoid daydreaming and mind wandering? How do you stay on the job without getting tired, fidgety, hungry, thirsty, distracted, or so frustrated that you put aside the work you need to do?

Why is it so difficult? What does it really take to be able to concentrate? Why is it so easy for some people and difficult for others? The answer to all of these questions can be found in each of the 4 categories listed below:

• *Purpose and Practicality*: The reason(s) for doing the assignment.

• *Interest*: The power of curiosity and personal benefit that you associate with an assignment.

• *Control*: Eliminating the conditions that cause most of the distractions.

• *Consequence I*: What happens when you fail to complete an assignment.

• *Consequence II*: What happens when you succeed.

Purpose and Practicality

Do you usually know why you are doing a particular assignment? For example, your Spanish teacher has assigned ten sentences that you have to translate from English to Spanish. Why? Is there some grammatical concept to practice in order to understand how to apply it? Is it to practice some new vocabulary words?

The enemy of concentration for this type of exercise is to think that there is no reason for the assignment, other than that the assignment is busy work. Following are typical assignments which include purposes and practical reasons for doing the work.

English Assignment: Read the Introduction to *JULIUS CAESAR* by Shakespeare. (Why? For what reasons?)

- To become familiar with the author and what life was like when he lived and wrote.

- To become familiar with the background of the play and the main characters.

- To become familiar with Shakespearean English in order to better understand the play.

- To learn how this play relates to the present day.

- To understand characterization.

- To understand the concept of "motivation," or why people behave the way they do.

- To gain greater appreciation of the English language.

- To learn something about Roman culture during the age of Caesar.

- To be better prepared for the action and the plot of the play.

Mathematics Assignment: Do 10 word problems dealing with percents and decimals. The purposes are:

- To recognize word problems as part of every day experience.

- To improve critical problem solving ability.

- To become familiar with the practical side of using percents and decimals.

- To become skilled in applying concepts.

- To demonstrate problem solving capability.

Social Studies Assignment: Read the chapter on "The Hopi Indians." The purposes are:

- To understand the Hopi social conditions and how their culture evolved.

- To appreciate Hopi artistic creations and how these relate to their culture.

- To understand the contemporary status of the Hopi and what this means to us.

- To appreciate the historical facts of Hopi contributions to the United States.

- To relate Hopi culture to other native American cultures.

- To find a topic for further research and a term paper.

Science Assignment: Start Unit on "Cells and Tissues." The purposes are:

- To learn the basic parts of a cell and how it lives.

- To understand the mechanics and principal parts of a microscope.

- To learn how to use the laboratory to investigate and verify scientific principles.

- To understand the process of cell division.

- To understand how DNA, RNA, and enzymes regulate the life activities of a cell.

- To understand the functions of tissues.

Foreign Language Assignment: Use of the Relative Pronoun. Translate ten English sentences into French. The purposes are:

- To demonstrate knowledge of what a Relative Pronoun is.

- To demonstrate knowledge of the forms of Relative Pronouns.

- To demonstrate ability to select the correct Relative Pronoun under all circumstances.

- To understand the pitfalls of English use of the Relative Pronoun compared to French use.

Notice that every one of the purposes listed on the preceding pages begins with the expression "*To*" do something. "*To* understand," "*To* learn," "*To* appreciate," "*To* demonstrate," "*To* become familiar with," and so on. All of these expressions imply being able to "perform" in some way or other as a result of the knowledge you gain from doing the assignment.

When you think of "purpose," always think of how it relates to "performance." Being able "*To do* something." Think of it this way:

First - You learn something (knowledge).

Next - You do something (purpose).

Last - You become something. (use).

Remember it this way:

> Know Something
>
> Do Something
>
> Be Something

23

PURPOSES - WORKSHEET

English

_____

_____

Social Studies

_____

_____

Math

_____

_____

Science

_____

_____

Foreign Language

_____

_____

Notes

_____

_____

_____

Interest In The Assignment

Interest in what you have to do is without a doubt the single most positive motivating force in getting you started and helping you keep your attention on your work. When interest is high, the time goes by quickly and you usually get a lot done. "But," you will probably ask, "how can I become interested in something I absolutely hate to do, like translating ten silly sentences from English into Spanish? What buttons do I press so that I can sit down and do the work?"

Unfortunately, there are no buttons to press. If your background and current knowledge of the subject are limited, this can be a drawback, especially in subjects like foreign language or mathematics. In these subjects, what you learn today is the building block for tomorrow's lesson. This is called cumulative knowledge.

You may be able to open a social studies book, an English book, and in many instances, a science book to any page and begin reading without any real difficulty. Not so in mathematics or foreign language. If you haven't thoroughly mastered Chapter One in these subjects, you cannot go on to Chapter Two. By the time you get to Chapter Five, the situation could become absolutely hopeless.

There is little or no way to become interested when you fall hopelessly behind in a subject. You will need other solutions such as special help from your teacher or a private tutor, or even a change in your program. The point I would like to stress is the importance of a *good beginning* in all classes, especially subjects that build like mathematics and foreign language.

But suppose you have a reasonably good background in a subject. What do you do then to become interested in a particular assignment? The following are some suggestions:

• *Make it fun* by using your imagination. In the case of the ten sentences to be translated from English to Spanish, try to make a story out of the sentences. The sillier the better.

Reword the math problems using far out expressions for all of the quantities, percents, or other parts of the problem.

If you are artistic, draw pictures or cartoons of the social studies assignment on the characteristics of the American voter. An added bonus is that this could be a big help to you when recalling the information. Think of what might happen if you changed a laboratory experiment in some bizarre way.

• *Make it a game*. Compete with yourself. Time yourself with a math problem and then try to do better with the next and the next. In a map exercise, plan it like a trip and give yourself points for different stops, and for knowing the names of places. How many points would you give Brutus for his big speech in **JULIUS CAESAR**? Marc Antony for his big speech? How would you calculate the points?

Try conjugating an irregular verb in five seconds, four seconds, three seconds.

Think of "trivia" questions as part of a science assignment.

Invent your own "games." Share them with your friends and teachers.

• *Make it relevant*. Try to develop as many relationships as you can between your work and your goals for the future. If you plan to study engineering, the more math and science you take, the better.

Associate your work with outside interests, a job, career, travel, hobbies, or current events.

●Use your knowledge for *potential profit*. Your knowledge of various subjects, particularly math, science and foreign languages, may qualify you to tutor other students for a fee. You not only make money, but you learn a lot. There is always a need for good tutors, and if you are good at it and like it, you might want to become a teacher.

●*Form a study group*. Get together with other students in the class to discuss the work, compare notes, and quiz each other.

●*Expand your knowledge*. Find other information on the subject using resources such as magazine articles, movies, TV programs, tapes, trips, lectures, etc. This will give you greater expertise and depth as well as heightened interest.

●*Make use of study aids*, such as *Cliff Notes*, summaries, outlines, translations, reviews, and other condensed forms of analysis and information. A warning, however, that you should be aware of is that the *study aid* is just that, an aid. It is not, I repeat, *not*, a substitute for what the teacher requires and expects you to do.

●*"Kill two birds with one stone."* If you are studying <u>JULIUS</u> <u>CAESAR</u> in your English class, and you are also doing a unit on Roman Civilization in your World History class, the two can benefit each other. Find ways for it to happen. The same goes for science, math, and many other combinations.

Knowledge does not exist in a vacuum. Always look for connections that can provide interest, save time, and provide you with greater understanding in your classes.

INTEREST - WORKSHEET

Use the suggestions I have given you about generating interest as a starting point for your own ideas. Think of how you might become more enthused about the work you have to do in each of your classes. Use imagination and creativity.

English

_____

_____

Social Studies

_____

_____

Math

_____

_____

Science

_____

_____

Foreign Language

_____

_____

Notes

_____

_____

Control

Your ability to concentrate also depends on your control of: internal, external, and organizational factors. Suppose we examine these separately.

INTERNAL CONTROL

This is really "self control." Who's in charge? You? Or something else? When you sit down to begin an assignment, is the stage set for work? Have you pre-arranged for distractions that will prevent you from doing your work? For example, consider the following questions before you get started on an important assignment:

- Are you *tired*?
- Are you *hungry*?
- Are you *thirsty*?
- Are you *hot*?
- Are you *cold*?
- Are you *cramped*?
- Are you *uncomfortable*?
- Are you *miserable*?
- Are you *excited*?
- Are you *anxious*?
- Are you *distraught*?

If you answered "Yes" to any of the above questions, you are not ready to begin concentrating on your assignments. Everything mentioned in the questions is something *you can control*. Don't sabotage yourself.

What can you do if you have any of the above *symptoms*? Step #1-Be *aware* of the condition. Be aware of what it could do to your ability to concentrate. Then before you get started, do whatever you can to eliminate the condition. Be as positive and effective as possible. Don't try to delude yourself. You can't concentrate when you lack sufficient *self control*.

EXTERNAL CONTROL

These are factors outside of yourself. You can control them, but they are not part of you personally. Remember, you can sabotage concentration as easily with external distractions as with internal ones. Don't let it happen. For example, consider what control you have over the following:

- The *study place*. Is it the best you can find?

- The *stereo*. How distracting is this to you when you study? Is it more distracting for some subjects, and less for others?

- Outside *noise*. How much can you tolerate? How much can you eliminate?

- The *lights*. Can you see well enough, or do you frequently have to strain your eyes?

- The *heat*. Can you control it? How much does it bother you?

- The *learning materials*. Is everything you need easily available?

When you consider all the possible internal and external types of distractions, you can quickly realize why it can be difficult to concentrate. The important thing is *for you to be in control.* You do this by confronting distractions head on, and not letting yourself be fooled or defeated.

ORGANIZATIONAL CONTROL

You are well organized when you can provide information for all of the categories listed below that are related to whatever assignment you may have.

DESCRIPTION
    How much are you required to do?
    What are you required to do?
    Where is it? Textbook? Workbook?
    When is it due?
    What *form* is required? Lined paper, pencil, pen?

TASKS
    Read
    Define
    Review
    Describe
    Solve
    Summarize

TEACHER EXPECTATIONS. Objectives?
    Demonstrate *skills*
    Be able to *use* and *apply* knowledge

TERMS and CONCEPTS
    Scientific
    Technical
    Grammatical
    Reference

MANAGING TIME
   Weekly Time Chart
   Assignment Log
   To-Do-List

RECALL
   Notetaking
   Mapping

TEST TAKING
   Preparation
   Taking the test

THE STUDY PLACE
   Quiet, conducive, orderly

   On the next page is a **WORKSHEET** on **CONTROL** factors. Examine your habits very carefully and decide what gives you the best possible control of everything that relates to doing your best work and completing all assignments on time.

(Umbrella diagram with panels labeled: DESCRIPTION, EXPECTATION, MATERIALS, TESTS, PLACE TO STUDY, TASKS, TIME, NOTES; handle spelling ORGANIZATION)

CONTROL - WORKSHEET

In the space below, list all the areas you need to control for the best possible concentration. Use the examples on he preceding two pages as a starting point. If you think of any others, list them also.

Internal or Self Control

_____

_____

_____

_____

External Control

_____

_____

_____

_____

Organizational Control

_____

_____

_____

_____

Consequence I
If Nothing Else Works

If all else fails, the last resort for improving your concentration is knowing what will happen if you don't do the work, or do it poorly. This is the "bottom line," the "fear factor," which also has its place in concentration.

The most obvious consequence of inability to concentrate on an assignment is failure. You fail a test, a class, or you might even fail to get a diploma. That's pretty powerful stuff, enough to motivate many students to get down to business. If, however, none of the consequences matter, and there are some students for whom there are no consequences, then the problems are outside the realm of this book. Surprisingly, there are many students who seldom take the trouble to think of consequences. If they did, the results could be quite different.

I never cease to be amazed when I ask a student why he or she has failed to turn in assignments and the answer is, "I forgot," or "I just didn't make time to do it," or other answers that indicate a real absence of any thought about the consequence of not doing the assignment.

In some ways, this relates to the first part of this section on *Purpose*. Many assignments are never done because students don't believe there is any real reason for doing them. The students may feel that some assignments are just "busy work," so why should they do them?

If you get in the habit of skipping assignments because they don't seem important, you might tend to see nearly all of your assignments that way. The consequences are obvious; don't let it happen to you. Use as much information in this Chapter as possible to help you succeed in everything you do.

Consequence II
Success Becomes A Habit

Now I want you to forget everything I said under **CONSEQUENCE I**, and think about *success*. What does it mean to you? What would happen if your teacher told you your work was among the best in the class? How would that affect your confidence? How would your parents react? Your friends? Do you think you can handle it? Of course you can.

Does it sound like a fantasy? It isn't. It can happen, and it will happen if you want it to, and if you are willing to believe it, work for it, and not let anything or anyone discourage you.

Remember, *success* like anything else, can become a habit, and when it does, it will be as difficult as any other habit to break. Think about what it will mean to you, and then *Go for it!*

Concentration - Summary

There are four basic factors that determine how well you can concentrate on your work:

PURPOSE and PRACTICALITY.

Why are you doing the assignment? What are the purposes, reasons, expectations and specific outcomes?

How will your work help you with whatever else you have to learn? How does it *fit in* to the overall requirements of the course?

INTEREST

How can you get interested in what you have to do? Some suggestions are:

Make it *fun*.
Make it a *game*.
Make it *relevant*.
Form a *study group*.
Expand your *knowledge*.
Use *study aids*.
"Kill two birds with one stone."

CONTROL FACTORS

Internal control means all the conditions within yourself that you can control such as being hungry, thirsty, tired, hot, cold, cramped, anxious, depressed, etc.

External control means the place, noise, lights, materials, etc.

Organizational control includes nine essential points to cover each time you get an assignment.

CONSEQUENCE I - *Failure*

What to expect if nothing mentioned above can be made to work.

CONSEQUENCE II - SUCCESS

What can happen if *success* becomes a *habit* you cannot break.

**California Education Plan, Inc.
Publishing Division**
4000 Middlefield Road • Palo Alto, CA 94303
Telephone: (415) 493-7070 or 493-5512

MOTIVATION & CONCENTRATION

Dear Reader:

We value your opinions. Your comments, criticisms, or suggestions will help our publications of tomorrow. If you have questions, you may expect an answer within one week.

Comments:

Criticism:

Suggestions:

Thank you for your help.

Herman Ohme

California Education Plan, Inc. - Publishing Division
4074 Fabian Way • Palo Alto, CA 94303
Telephone: (415) 493-7070 or 493-5512

ORDER FORM

Please send the following books by Herman Ohme:

Quantity	Title	Price
_____	"Learn How To Learn STUDY SKILLS	$11.95
_____	Teacher Guide to STUDY SKILLS	2.95
_____	Parent Guide	3.95
_____	Organization & Time Management	3.95
_____	Motivation & Concentration	3.95
_____	Notetaking & Report Preparation	3.95
_____	Test Taking	3.95
_____	Foreign Language Skills & Grammatical Glossary	4.95
_____	Complete Set (All of the Above)	39.60

Name (please print) _____

Address _____

City _____ State _____ ZIP _____

Amount _____ ☐Check ☐VISA ☐M/C Card # _____

Signature _____ Exp. Date _____

Californians: Add 7% Sales Tax

Shipping & Handling: U.S., 10%--Outside the U.S., 20% plus duty

4 What did Malone find when he got back to the camp?
5 Who did Malone go and speak to?

9

1 Roxton told Malone what had happened in the camp. What had happened?
2 Where did Malone and Roxton go? What did they see?
3 How was Summerlee saved from the Ape-People?
4 Who followed the explorers back to their camp?

10

1 What happened to Malone on the way to the Indians' caves?
2 What did the explorers find out about the young Indian?
3 How were the explorers going to help the Indians?
4 What did the explorers find out about the iguanodons?
5 Who won the battle on the plateau?

11

1 Why were the Indians safe in their caves?
2 One day Malone saw something strange at the pterodactyl pit. What was it?
3 Who helped the explorers leave the Lost World? How did he help them?
4 How did the explorers get out of the Lost World?

12

1 What did Professor Summerlee tell the audience in the Zoological Institute?
2 What did Dr Illingworth ask Professor Challenger to do?
3 What had Professor Challenger brought from the Lost World? What did it do?
4 Why did people now believe in the Lost World?

Heinemann English Language Teaching
A division of Reed Educational and Professional Publishing Limited
Halley Court, Jordan Hill, Oxford OX2 8EJ

OXFORD MADRID FLORENCE ATHENS PRAGUE
SÃO PAULO MEXICO CITY CHICAGO PORTSMOUTH (NH)
TOKYO SINGAPORE KUALA LUMPUR MELBOURNE
AUCKLAND JOHANNESBURG IBADAN GABORONE

SBN 0 435 27318 3

This retold version for Heinemann Guided Readers
Text © Anne Collins 1995
Design and illustration © Heinemann Publishers (Oxford) Ltd 1995
First published 1995

All rights reserved; no part of this publication may be
reproduced, stored in a retrieval system, transmitted in any
form, or by any means, electronic, mechanical, photocopying,
recording, or otherwise, without the prior written permission of
the publishers.

Illustrated by Kathy Stephen
Typography by Adrian Hodgkins
Designed by Sue Vaudin
Cover by Graham Humphreys and Marketplace Design
Set in 11.5/14.5 Goudy
Printed and bound in Malta